CRIMCOMICS

SUBCULTURAL THEORIES

KRISTA S. GEHRING

WRITER

MICHAEL R. BATISTA

ARTIST

CHERYL L. WALLACE

LETTERER

New York   Oxford

OXFORD UNIVERSITY PRESS

FOREWORD

A review of some of the most popular DC and Marvel action comics reveals a timeless storyline: an otherworldly champion of ordinary citizens—the superhero, who possess extraordinary abilities, battles a villain intent on casting troubles for orderly society. The citizens support the superhero but abhor the villain. The defeat of the villain is a defeat of his harmful ideas. And this saga continues in another form in a different story. Evil continuously simmers beneath the conventional world.

I read widely and often, and have since I was a young child, but I do not recall ever reading a comic book from cover to cover. Still, I have always been aware of their popularity and significance. After all, the comic book superheroes are so ingrained in the fabric of American culture that one comes to know them eventually. Much like any alluring form of fiction, comics seem to serve some transcendent purpose for all of us. I have come to realize that fiction, however it appears, is an incredibly powerful art form.

What can the popularity of the hero and villain narrative in comic books teach students about academic criminology? We are drawn to the writer's imagination perhaps because it serves our curiosities. Perhaps

comic books reaffirm the boundaries of acceptable and unacceptable behavior. So often the heroic protagonist embodies the moral character a society seems to find most redeemable. The antagonist is a vehicle to express our contempt for those who cannot conform to conventional rules. Maybe the stories do even more than this for the reader: Their powerful appeal might reflect our interests in understanding why someone would pursue acts of lawlessness and violence. The solution for us is to overpower the wrongdoer with a champion of good.

Perpetrating acts of serious crime, particularly violence, is inconceivable to the vast majority of people. Citizens wonder, who could commit so much harm with so little regard for the well-being of others and themselves? They wonder, too, how is it that certain neighborhoods or street segments consistently experience elevated rates of serious and deadly violence, year after year, whereas other areas in the same city are virtually free of crime? Criminological theory provides an answer to these questions in the literature on subcultural differentiation. This literature all but abandons the calculus found in the classical school in favor of substantive positivism.

Most people abide by conventional conduct norms where inflicting harm on a fellow citizen is sternly condemned. Perhaps the near universal acceptance of these norms is why violence is uncommon. But the United States is a large, highly populated, economically stratified, and culturally heterogeneous nation in which contradictory norms about right and wrong coexist with the normative standards of the majority culture. According to theorists, acts of serious crime are fundamentally determined by norms espoused in subcultures. To this end, murder, robbery, assault, and burglary are committed by a faction of individuals who are socialized to believe in a different version of the cultural system that constitutes the social order. These acts in particular are expressions of norms that sanction patterns of conduct in direct conflict with the behavioral standards endorsed by the majority group.

The subcultural perspective can be illustrated in simple allegory: Just as using a fork to eat a meal is compelled by norms, so are acts of criminal behavior. The person who eats his salad with a fork does so almost reflexively. Likewise, the person who physically assaults another man for disrespecting also does so reflexively. Obviously, this allegory is a gross simplification of the underlying theoretical logic. Nonetheless, a key point is that most behaviors are deemed appropriate insofar as they remain consistent with the norms of the group to which the individual belongs. The behavior is deviant from the perspective of members of the external group because it violates *their* rules.

Large-scale structural changes figure importantly in theories of subcultural differentiation. Around the early 20th century, when the original subcultural perspectives were conceived, the United States was experiencing the dual forces of waves of immigration from European countries along with the transition from an agrarian to an industrial economy. The impact of these forces was largely concentrated in urban areas where, together, they led to dramatic expansions of the residential populations of Midwestern and Northern cities such as Chicago,

Philadelphia, and St. Louis. Never before were so many people from so many different regions of the world brought together in densely inhabited and often impoverished urban areas.

The changing profile of America's cities brought a number of challenges for civic life, and though they were not necessarily new challenges, they were now on a much larger scale. Youth crime was an especially thorny problem.

In what was perhaps then seen as an empirical breakthrough, criminologists of the early 20th century established that delinquency was disproportionately located in a small number of neighborhoods located around the city center. Its spatial persistence seemed to emerge from the process of cultural transmission, whereby older generations communicated to younger generations the norms of the delinquent subculture. Naturally, early subcultural research was intensely focused on youth gangs as reservoirs of subcultural norms. Delinquency certainly was not exclusive to working-class boys affiliated with criminal peer groups. But the persistent concentration of delinquency among low-income youth residing in impoverished immigrant communities furnished gang researchers with ample evidence to believe their delinquency was of a particular form practiced in localized groups and contrived as a solution to collective problems. To the early generation of subcultural scholars, the lower-class gang was the delinquent subculture *par excellence*.

Subcultural theory continued to evolve. Strain theory provided the logical bridge between the class structure and the formation of the gang and its alternative conduct norms. Moreover, theorists recognized that to understand the nature of gangs, and thus their normative structures, one must account for the qualities of the local neighborhoods in which they are situated.

Since the 1980s, the focus of subcultural theory has gradually shifted away from concerns with youth gangs and general delinquency to an interest in the cultural transmission of violent conduct norms independent of gang participation. Researchers came to realize that gangs were not the sole conduits of subcultural orientations.

New perspectives were developed in the wake of the deindustrialization of America's cities. Neighborhoods were no longer localized immigrant enclaves. Cities were no longer the engines of productivity and upward economic mobility as they once were in the early 20th century. Rather, urban areas were beset by pernicious conditions of unemployment, racial segregation, impotent public resources, and pervasive poverty. Emerging from this tangle of disadvantage is what Anderson described as the street code—a contemporary subcultural orientation intensely concerned with self-preservation.

Part of my career has been spent testing the logical assumptions of various subcultural models. The street code thesis is the most studied subcultural perspective in contemporary academic criminology. From my own assessment, it has reasonably strong empirical support. The street code perspective seems to account for the facts about the distribution of serious and lethal violence. Some might find that it provides a somewhat satisfactory answer to questions about the social foundations of lethal violence in America's cities.

Informed skepticism is a healthy quality. Subcultural theory is not immune to scientific criticism. Some criminologists doubt whether subcultural conduct norms are authentic. Some even question the assumptions about human nature underlying subcultural theory. Others believe the very term subculture implies far too much normative consensus. Few would doubt, however, the enduring significance of this theoretical tradition to the criminological canon.

The present edition of *CrimComics* carefully and masterfully charts the intellectual history of subcultural theory in criminology beginning with the period of urban social upheaval in the early 20th century to the present day. The comic builds for the reader a vivid portrait of the links between the evolving assumptions of the various conceptual models and the developing structural, cultural, and political circumstances of the times. The writing of Krista Gehring and the visual artistry of Michael Batista create clever stories in which the main assumptions of each perspective unfold as narrated dialogue. The authors do not spare fundamental details. Front and center in every story are two especially useful components: the background of the scholar who authored the theory and the historical period in which the theory emerged. Somehow, skillfully, the storylines of each theory coalesce into a common narrative of explanation that any serious student of criminology is sure to appreciate.

This issue of *CrimComics* is enjoyable to read and absolutely engaging. It certainly will be a valuable tool for classroom instruction.

MARK T. BERG
University of Iowa

PREFACE

When I conduct research for an issue of *CrimComics*, I am always amazed at how many criminological theories developed by "standing on the shoulders of giants." Discovering the connection between many of these criminologists is like creating a very elaborate "family tree" that illustrates who influenced the ideas of whom. This is very apparent in the current issue, as ideas from the Chicago School of Criminology (see *CrimComics: Social Disorganization Theory*) and Robert Merton (see *CrimComics: Anomie and Strain Theories*) combined to produce two subcultural theories that emerged in the 1950s and 1960s. I can't help but marvel at how chance meetings greatly influenced criminological theory.

Interest in youth gangs occurred after World War II as this segment of the population grew and their activities became more prominent. At this time, several scholars wrote about juvenile gangs from very different perspectives. It is in these academic legacies that the connections and influences of so many different theorists become apparent. When I write *CrimComics*, I love to delve into the biographies of the scholars who produced these theories. When I do so, I try to incorporate some interesting anecdote or characteristic that perhaps a student reading about these theorists would not know. When I discovered that Albert Cohen was denied admission into several graduate schools for a rather sinister reason, this provided the basis of a rich story of his rather serendipitous journey through academic life. It is clear that his classes with Robert Merton, along with

his chance meeting with Edwin Sutherland, shaped his theorizing about juvenile gangs. But what if he had never received that telegram from Sutherland?

A similar situation contributed to the development of Differential Opportunity Theory by Richard Cloward and Lloyd Ohlin. Cloward was a student of Robert Merton's at Columbia University while Ohlin studied under Edwin Sutherland and later got his doctorate at the University of Chicago. They met, by chance, when they were both social work faculty at Columbia University. What if that meeting had never occurred?

Another interesting connection I made while writing this issue was that Cohen and Walter Miller developed their theories of juvenile gangs in a rather synchronous manner. In 1955, Cohen proposed that gangs were a response to youth feeling status frustration because they were not able to "measure up" to the "middle-class measuring rod." Gangs were an adaptation for these youth to engage in activities they would be able to achieve. *In the very same city, during the same time period,* Miller (1957) provided a very different explanation of juvenile gangs. He did not believe, as Cohen did, that lower-class culture and gangs were a response to mainstream culture. He felt that lower-class culture was distinct and stood on its own. While Cohen remained in the halls of Harvard crafting his theory by building upon the extant literature produced by the Chicago School and Robert Merton, Miller developed his theory through his observations walking the streets of the Roxbury neighborhood south of Cambridge. What would have happened if they had crossed paths?

As with any book project, *CrimComics* consumed much time and effort, perhaps more so than a traditional textbook. Thinking about theory—and, in particular, trying to design a work that best conveys the theories in a visual medium—is fun. Still, with busy lives, finding the space in one's day to carefully research, write, illustrate, ink, and letter the pages of this work is a source of some stress. We were fortunate, however, to have had an amazing amount of support during these times from family, friends, and Oxford University Press. We also want to acknowledge the talents of Cheryl Wallace. Cheryl's flair for lettering allowed us to get our ideas across to the readers.

The support of these and so many other individuals has made creating *CrimComics* possible and a rewarding experience for us. We would like to thank the following reviewers: Thomas Chuda, Bunker Hill Community College; Tara N. Richards, University of Baltimore; Paul Nunis, Arkansas State University; Kim DeTardo-Bora, Marshall University; Jess Bonnan-White, Stockton University; Elizabeth Perkins, Morehead State University; Dennis Breslin, University of Connecticut–Avery Point; Charles Crawford, Western Michigan University; Cedric Michel, The University of Tampa; Anna Divita, UNC Charlotte. We hope that this and other issues of *CrimComics* will inspire in your students a passion to learn criminological theory.

Subcultural Theories

IN AN INDUSTRIALIZED SOCIETY LIKE THE UNITED STATES, THERE IS A GREAT DEAL OF CULTURAL DIVERSITY.

THIS CULTURAL DIVERSITY FACILITATES THE DEVELOPMENT OF NUMEROUS *SUBCULTURES*.

SUBCULTURES ARE THOSE GROUPS THAT HAVE VALUES AND NORMS DISTINCT FROM THOSE HELD BY THE MAJORITY.

THEY OFTEN FORGE A LIFESTYLE DIFFERENT FROM THE MAINSTREAM CULTURE AND ARE OFTEN AT ODDS WITH IT.

FOR EXAMPLE, IN THE UNITED STATES, SUBCULTURES MIGHT INCLUDE HIPPIES, GOTHS, ROLE-PLAYING GAMERS, AND BIKERS.

AN AREA OF PARTICULAR INTEREST FOR SOME CRIMINOLOGISTS IS *DELINQUENT SUBCULTURES*.

SPECIFICALLY, *GANGS*.

GANGS EMERGED IN AMERICAN CITIES AS LARGE INFLUXES OF IMMIGRANTS ARRIVED TO THESE URBAN CENTERS.

WHEN THESE INDIVIDUALS ARRIVED, THERE WERE FEW OPTIONS FOR THEM.

CHICAGO WAS AN URBAN CENTER IN WHICH THE EMERGENCE OF THESE GANGS WAS ONE CONTRIBUTOR TO THE RISE IN CRIME RATES IN CERTAIN AREAS OF THE CITY.

MANY HAD TO LIVE IN SQUALID, OVERCROWDED SLUMS AND WERE SUBJECTED TO INTENSE COMPETITION FOR JOBS.

THIS ALSO HAPPENED TO BE THE LOCATION OF THE UNIVERSITY OF CHICAGO WITH THE COUNTRY'S OLDEST SOCIOLOGY DEPARTMENT...

...SO THIS WAS A PRIME LOCATION TO STUDY THESE GANGS IN A "NATURAL SETTING."

MANY SCHOLARS IN THIS DEPARTMENT WERE TRYING TO EXPLAIN CRIMINAL ACTIVITY IN INNER-CITY CHICAGO AND WHAT SUSTAINED IT.*

THOSE IDEAS, OFTEN REFERRED TO THE *CHICAGO SCHOOL* OF THOUGHT, WOULD INFLUENCE MANY SUBSEQUENT SCHOLARS.

*CHECK OUT CRIMCOMICS: SOCIAL DISORGANIZATION THEORY FOR MORE INFORMATION ABOUT THIS!

HARVARD UNIVERSITY, 1937.

SOMETIMES CRIMINOLOGICAL THEORISTS ARE "SINGULARLY FORTUNATE" IN THAT THEY ARE EXPOSED TO INFLUENTIAL SCHOLARS DURING THEIR ACADEMIC PURSUITS.

WHILE A SOPHOMORE AT HARVARD UNIVERSITY, COHEN TOOK AN INTRODUCTORY SOCIOLOGY COURSE TAUGHT BY PITRIM SOROKIN, A VERY WELL KNOWN SOCIOLOGIST AT THE TIME.

ANY ORGANIZED SOCIAL GROUP IS ALWAYS A STRATIFIED SOCIAL BODY.

THERE HAS NOT BEEN AND DOES NOT EXIST ANY PERMANENT SOCIAL GROUP THAT IS "FLAT" AND IN WHICH ALL MEMBERS ARE EQUAL.

THIS RESULTED IN HIS "CONVERSION" TO SOCIOLOGY.

HE WAS INTOXICATED BY THE IDEAS OF SOCIAL SYSTEMS AND CULTURES.

SUCH WAS THE CASE FOR ALBERT COHEN.

HIS JUNIOR YEAR, HE TOOK A COURSE ABOUT SOCIAL INSTITUTIONS WITH TALCOTT PARSONS, ANOTHER VERY INFLUENTIAL SOCIOLOGIST.

EVERY SOCIAL SYSTEM IS A FUNCTIONING ENTITY.

SENIOR YEAR, HE TOOK A COURSE IN SOCIAL ORGANIZATION FROM ROBERT MERTON,* PERHAPS THE MOST FAMOUS SOCIOLOGIST OF THE 20TH CENTURY.

THE EXTREME EMPHASIS UPON THE ACCUMULATION OF WEALTH AS A SYMBOL OF SUCCESS IN OUR SOCIETY WEAKENS EFFECTIVE CONTROL OF INSTITUTIONALLY REGULATED MODES OF ACQUIRING A FORTUNE.

*FIND OUT MORE ABOUT ROBERT MERTON IN CRIMCOMICS: ANOMIE AND STRAIN THEORIES!

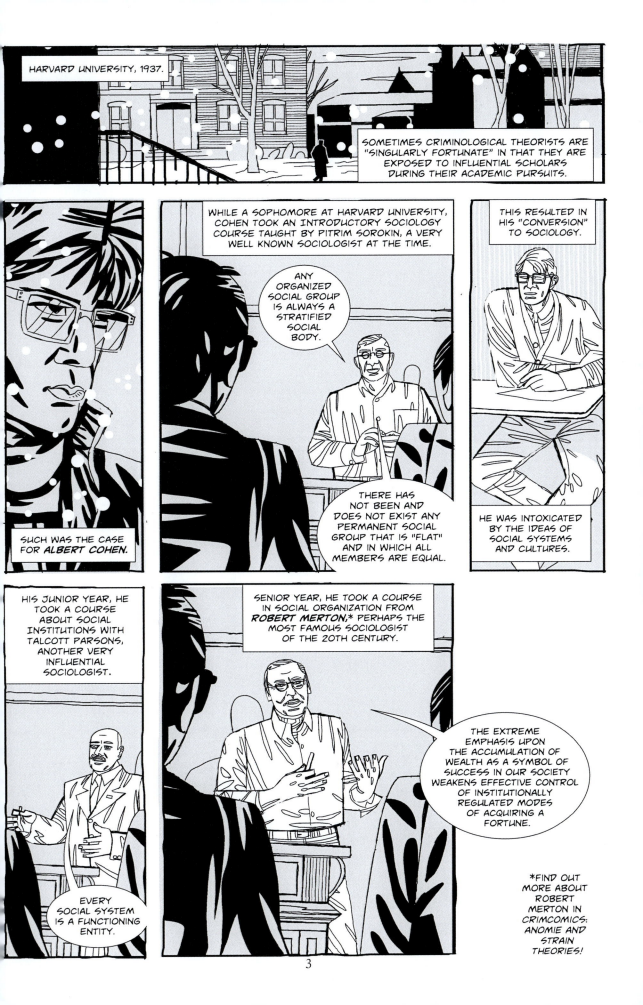

3

THIS LAST-MINUTE INVITATION TO STUDY AT INDIANA UNIVERSITY BLOOMINGTON PROVED TO BE ONE MORE IN THAT SERIES OF "SINGULARLY FORTUNATE" EVENTS THAT PROPELLED COHEN INTO THE FIELD OF CRIMINOLOGY.

COHEN WAS ABLE TO TAKE CLASSES FROM *EDWIN SUTHERLAND* WHILE AT INDIANA UNIVERSITY BLOOMINGTON.

IN 1913, SUTHERLAND RECEIVED HIS DOCTORATE FROM THE UNIVERSITY OF CHICAGO AND WAS A RESEARCH PROFESSOR THERE BEFORE EVENTUALLY GOING TO INDIANA UNIVERSITY BLOOMINGTON.

WHILE AT CHICAGO, HE WAS EXPOSED TO THE IDEAS OF THE CHICAGO SCHOOL REGARDING CRIME RATES IN THE CITY, AND BEFRIENDED A COLORFUL INDIVIDUAL NAMED BROADWAY JONES.

JONES WAS A GRIFTER AND A CON MAN, AND HE WOULD TELL ME THE MOST INTERESTING AND HARROWING STORIES ABOUT HIS CRIMINAL EXPLOITS.

THAT IS WHEN I CAME TO THE CONCLUSION THAT PROFESSIONAL CRIMINALS LEARN THE TECHNIQUES AND ATTITUDES ASSOCIATED WITH THEIR WORK FROM CLOSE RELATIONSHIPS WITH OTHER PROFESSIONAL CRIMINALS.

THIS WAS DONE IN THE CONTEXT OF A DELINQUENT SUBCULTURE, LIKE A GANG.

EDWIN, YOU HAVE TALKED A LOT ABOUT DELINQUENT SUBCULTURES AND HOW YOUTH LEARN FROM ONE ANOTHER...

...BUT WHERE DO THE SUBCULTURES COME FROM?

I'M NOT SURE WHAT YOU MEAN, AL. THESE SUBCULTURES TEND TO BE LOCATED IN SLUM AREAS.

WHAT I'VE BEEN TALKING ABOUT EXPLAINS HOW ONE YOUTH CAN BE DELINQUENT WHILE ANOTHER IS NOT--IT DEPENDS ON THEIR DIFFERENTIAL ASSOCIATIONS WITH DELINQUENT VERSUS LAW-ABIDING YOUTH.

BUT WHERE DO THE SUBCULTURES COME FROM? HOW DID THEY ORIGINATE? AND WHY ARE THEY LOCATED IN SLUM AREAS?

YES, I GET THAT. AND THAT EXPLAINS DELINQUENCY ON AN INDIVIDUAL LEVEL.

THIS QUESTIONING REFLECTED COHEN'S EXPOSURE TO IDEAS ABOUT SOCIAL STRUCTURES AND *MACRO-LEVEL* THEORIZING AT HARVARD UNIVERSITY.

BECAUSE SUTHERLAND FOCUSED MORE ON *SOCIAL PSYCHOLOGY* AND *MICRO-LEVEL* EXPLANATIONS OF BEHAVIOR, HE WAS NOT ABLE TO ANSWER COHEN'S INQUIRIES.

COHEN WAS EXPLORING A NEW WAY TO THINK ABOUT THESE SUBCULTURES.

HARVARD UNIVERSITY, 1946.

COHEN RETURNED TO HARVARD FOR HIS DOCTORATE AND ADDRESSED THESE QUESTIONS IN HIS DISSERTATION.

IN ADDITION TO HIS EXPOSURE TO VERY INFLUENTIAL SCHOLARS, IT IS LIKELY THAT COHEN'S THEORIZING WAS GREATLY INFLUENCED BY MANY SOCIO-POLITICAL EVENTS HAPPENING AT THE TIME.

THE SECOND WORLD WAR HAD ENDED A YEAR PRIOR TO HIS ADMISSION TO HARVARD, AND PEOPLE WERE ADJUSTING TO A SOCIETY THAT WAS NOT AT WAR.

THE 1944 GI BILL PROVIDED RETURNING VETERANS WITH MONEY FOR COLLEGE, BUSINESSES, AND HOME MORTGAGES.

SUDDENLY, MILLIONS OF SERVICEMEN WERE ABLE TO AFFORD HOMES OF THEIR OWN FOR THE FIRST TIME.

THEN CAME THE CARS, THE BACKYARD BARBECUES, THE BLACK-AND-WHITE TVS, THE APPLIANCES--ALL MANNER OF ITEMS WERE AVAILABLE FOR PURCHASE.

PEOPLE HAD MONEY TO SPEND, AND MORE AND MORE ITEMS TO SPEND IT ON.

OUR MODERN IMAGE OF THE *MIDDLE CLASS* COMES FROM THIS TIME PERIOD IN THE UNITED STATES' HISTORY.

INFLUENCED BY THIS, COHEN PROPOSED THERE WAS A "DOMINANT CULTURE" IN THE UNITED STATES THAT ASCRIBED TO MIDDLE-CLASS VALUES.

SINCE A DOMINANT CULTURE EXISTS, THIS IMPLIES OTHER SUBCULTURES EXIST AS WELL, EACH SUBSCRIBING TO THEIR OWN CULTURAL VALUES.

THIS IS MOST APPARENT IN SCHOOL SETTINGS, AS THIS IS WHERE THE VALUES OF THE DOMINANT CULTURE ARE TAUGHT.

IT IS ALSO WHERE THE VALUES CELEBRATED BY THE DOMINANT CULTURE CLASH WITH THE STRUCTURAL POSITIONS OF THOSE OF THE LOWER AND WORKING CLASS.

IN SCHOOL, BOYS ARE JUDGED IN RELATION TO MIDDLE-CLASS VALUES SUCH AS AMBITION, CONSTRUCTIVE USE OF LEISURE TIME, CULTIVATION OF SKILLS, INDIVIDUAL RESPONSIBILITY, AND DELAYED GRATIFICATION.

SPELLING BEE CHAMPION

THESE VALUES CONSTITUTE WHAT COHEN DESCRIBED AS THE *MIDDLE-CLASS MEASURING ROD*.

COHEN PROPOSED THAT BOYS COMING FROM THE WORKING CLASS WERE AT A DISADVANTAGE TO GAIN STATUS ACCORDING TO THE MIDDLE-CLASS MEASURING ROD.

FAILURE TO ACHIEVE STATUS LEADS THE YOUTH TO FEEL *STATUS FRUSTRATION* WHEN THEY SUFFER A PROBLEM OF ADJUSTMENT CAUSED BY FAILURE AT SCHOOL.

ULTIMATELY, COHEN'S DISSERTATION COMBINED THE CONCEPTS PROPOSED BY TWO SCHOOLS OF THOUGHT TO EXPLAIN DELINQUENT SUBCULTURE.

FIRST, HE EMPLOYED THE CONCEPT OF **STRAIN** THAT WAS PROPOSED BY ROBERT MERTON.

THESE BOYS FELT STRAIN BECAUSE THEY COULD NOT MEASURE UP TO MIDDLE-CLASS VALUES.

SECOND, AS THE CHICAGO THEORISTS (INCLUDING EDWIN SUTHERLAND) TAUGHT, THIS CRIMINAL CULTURE CAN BE TRANSMITTED TO YOUTHS IN THE NEIGHBORHOOD.

THUS, **CULTURAL TRANSMISSION** OF CRIMINAL TRADITIONS ALSO CAME INTO PLAY IN THE DEVELOPMENT OF JUVENILE GANGS.

IN 1955 COHEN PUBLISHED A REVISED VERSION OF HIS DISSERTATION TITLED DELINQUENT BOYS: THE CULTURE OF THE GANG.

MEANWHILE, ACROSS TOWN...

WHILE ALBERT COHEN WAS THEORIZING ABOUT DELINQUENT GANGS INSIDE THE WALLS OF HARVARD UNIVERSITY IN CAMBRIDGE, MASSACHUSETTS...

...*WALTER MILLER* WAS WALKING THE STREETS OF THE ROXBURY NEIGHBORHOOD, CONTACTING SOCIAL WORKERS AND LOCAL GANG MEMBERS AS PART OF THE BOSTON *SPECIAL YOUTH PROGRAM (SYP)*.

THIS PROGRAM WAS INITIATED BY A HORRIBLE EVENT SEVERAL YEARS EARLIER...

ON NEW YEAR'S EVE OF 1952, A RABBI WAS MURDERED IN ROXBURY.

NEWS REPORTS INDICATED A MUGGING HAD ESCALATED TO A MURDER AND THE SUSPECTS WERE GANG MEMBERS FROM A LOCAL HOUSING PROJECT.

THIS INCIDENT AFFIRMED LOCAL RESIDENTS' PERCEPTION THAT THERE WAS A GROWING PROBLEM OF DELINQUENCY AND GANG ACTIVITY.

THEY FORMED A COMMITTEE TO ADDRESS THIS ISSUE, AND RECEIVED FEDERAL FUNDING TO COORDINATE THE FIRST FEDERALLY FUNDED GANG STUDY, THE SPECIAL YOUTH PROGRAM.

IDEAS CAUSE REACTIONS.

THE STUDY BEGAN IN THE SUMMER OF 1954, WITH THE PURPOSE TO EVALUATE THE EFFICACY OF OUT-REACH WORKER PROGRAMS. WALTER MILLER WAS NAMED DIRECTOR OF THE PROGRAM.

AS PART OF THE PROGRAM, HE AND SEVERAL TRAINED SOCIAL WORKERS MAINTAINED CONTACT WITH TWENTY-ONE CORNER GROUP GANGS IN ROXBURY.

THE GOALS OF THE PROGRAM WERE TO GUIDE GANG MEMBERS TO MORE PROSOCIAL ACTIVITIES, PROVIDE SERVICES TO FAMILIES, AND GIVE THE COMMUNITY TOOLS TO HELP CONTROL DELINQUENCY WHEN THE STUDY WAS COMPLETE.

MILLER ALSO PLAYED A MEAN TRUMPET AND USED HIS MUSICAL TALENT AS A WAY TO CONNECT WITH THE GANG YOUTH HE WORKED WITH.

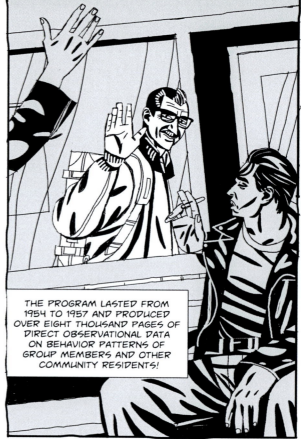

THE PROGRAM LASTED FROM 1954 TO 1957 AND PRODUCED OVER EIGHT THOUSAND PAGES OF DIRECT OBSERVATIONAL DATA ON BEHAVIOR PATTERNS OF GROUP MEMBERS AND OTHER COMMUNITY RESIDENTS!

CONTRARY TO WHAT SEVERAL SCHOLARS AT THE TIME BELIEVED (LIKE COHEN, AND CLOWARD AND OHLIN DISCUSSED LATER), MILLER DID NOT BELIEVE THAT YOUTH IN LOWER INCOME AREAS JOINED GANGS AS AN ADAPTATION TO NOT "MAKING IT" IN MAINSTREAM CULTURE.

MILLER BELIEVED THAT GANG MEMBERS WERE ADOLESCENTS ENGAGING IN THE NORMAL BEHAVIORS OF THEIR COMMUNITIES.

HE ASSERTED THAT LOWER-CLASS CULTURE AS A WHOLE--NOT SUBCULTURES WITHIN LOWER-CLASS AREAS-- IS RESPONSIBLE FOR GENERATING CRIMINALITY IN URBAN AREAS.

HE SAW EVIDENCE THAT SUPPORTED A DISTINCTIVE LOWER-CLASS CULTURAL SYSTEM CHARACTERIZED BY A SET OF SIX *FOCAL CONCERNS*.

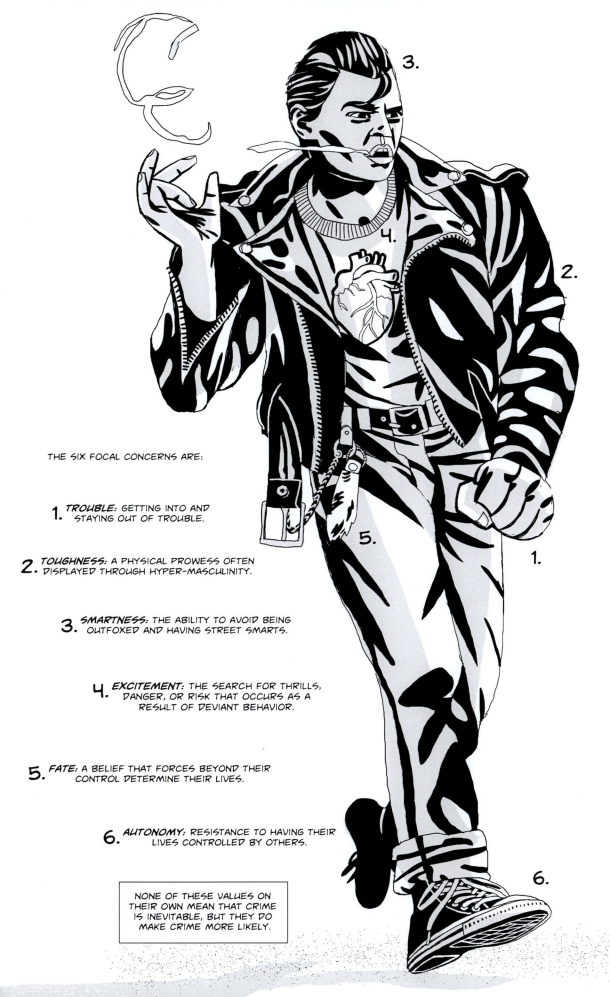

THE SIX FOCAL CONCERNS ARE:

1. *TROUBLE:* GETTING INTO AND
   STAYING OUT OF TROUBLE.

2. *TOUGHNESS:* A PHYSICAL PROWESS OFTEN
   DISPLAYED THROUGH HYPER-MASCULINITY.

3. *SMARTNESS:* THE ABILITY TO AVOID BEING
   OUTFOXED AND HAVING STREET SMARTS.

4. *EXCITEMENT:* THE SEARCH FOR THRILLS,
   DANGER, OR RISK THAT OCCURS AS A
   RESULT OF DEVIANT BEHAVIOR.

5. *FATE:* A BELIEF THAT FORCES BEYOND THEIR
   CONTROL DETERMINE THEIR LIVES.

6. *AUTONOMY:* RESISTANCE TO HAVING THEIR
   LIVES CONTROLLED BY OTHERS.

NONE OF THESE VALUES ON
THEIR OWN MEAN THAT CRIME
IS INEVITABLE, BUT THEY DO
MAKE CRIME MORE LIKELY.

MILLER'S WORK IS DISTINGUISHED FROM THAT OF OTHER SCHOLARS INTERESTED IN GANGS AT THIS TIME IN THAT 1) IT DID NOT DRAW FROM PROMINENT SOCIOLOGICAL THEORIES OF DELINQUENCY AT THE TIME AND 2) IT WAS BASED ON OBSERVATIONAL DATA.

TWO OF THOSE "OTHER SCHOLARS" WERE RICHARD CLOWARD AND LLOYD OHLIN. LIKE ALBERT COHEN, THEY WERE INFLUENCED BY HOW VERY PROMINENT THEORISTS THOUGHT ABOUT JUVENILE GANGS.

THEY MET ONE ANOTHER WHEN THEY WERE SOCIAL WORK FACULTY MEMBERS AT COLUMBIA AND ENTERED INTO A COLLABORATION THAT PRODUCED *DIFFERENTIAL OPPORTUNITY THEORY*.

OHLIN STUDIED UNDER EDWIN SUTHERLAND AND LATER EARNED HIS DOCTORATE AT THE UNIVERSITY OF CHICAGO.

CLOWARD HAD BEEN A STUDENT OF ROBERT MERTON AT COLUMBIA UNIVERSITY.

THIS THEORY WAS TIMELY, AS THE DECADE OF THE 1960S SAW INCREASING ATTENTION GIVEN TO THE ISSUE OF SOCIAL AND ECONOMIC INEQUALITY.

PRESIDENT JOHN F. KENNEDY SPOKE OF A "NEW FRONTIER," WHILE LYNDON B. JOHNSON CALLED FOR A "GREAT SOCIETY" AND A "WAR ON POVERTY."

THE CIVIL RIGHTS MOVEMENT WAS GAINING TRACTION AND WOULD SOON CAPTURE THE ATTENTION OF THE ENTIRE COUNTRY.

IT WAS THE PERFECT TIME FOR A BOOK THAT LINKED DELINQUENCY TO DISADVANTAGED YOUTHS' DENIAL OF OPPORTUNITY.

15

IT HAD BEEN ESTABLISHED THAT LOWER-CLASS YOUTH EXPERIENCED HIGH LEVELS OF STRAIN AND THUS ENGAGED IN DELINQUENCY.

WHAT HAD NOT BEEN EXPLAINED WAS WHY SUBCULTURAL RESPONSES OF A PARTICULAR TYPE EMERGED.

CLOWARD AND OHLIN PROPOSED THAT DELINQUENT SUBCULTURES COULD EMERGE IN AREAS WHERE THERE WERE ENOUGH YOUTHS TO COME TOGETHER AND TO SUPPORT EACH OTHER'S ALIENATION FROM CONVENTIONAL VALUES.

THEY ALSO SAID THE TYPE OF COLLECTIVE RESPONSE OR ADAPTATION TO THIS WOULD BE SHAPED BY THE NEIGHBORHOOD IN WHICH THEY LIVED.

THERE WERE THREE DIFFERENT SUBCULTURES THAT YOUNG PEOPLE MIGHT ENTER INTO:

CRIMINAL SUBCULTURES TEND TO EMERGE IN ORGANIZED SLUM AREAS WHERE THERE ARE CRIMINAL ROLE MODELS FOR YOUNG PEOPLE.

THESE OLDER OFFENDERS TEACH YOUTH HOW TO ENGAGE IN ILLEGAL CRIMINAL ENTERPRISES. THEY TYPICALLY COMMIT CRIMES THAT YIELD FINANCIAL REWARDS.

MR. CICCONE? I WANT YOU TO MEET MY FRIEND KENNY.

IN DISORGANIZED NEIGHBORHOODS, ACCESS TO THESE CRIMINAL "APPRENTICESHIPS" DOES NOT EXIST.

WITHOUT THE OPPORTUNITY TO EMBARK ON MORE LUCRATIVE ILLEGAL CRIMINAL CAREERS, THE YOUTHS HERE TURN TO VIOLENCE AS A WAY TO ESTABLISH A "REP" OR SOCIAL STATUS.

HERE, CONDITIONS ARE IDEAL FOR THE EMERGENCE OF A *CONFLICT SUBCULTURE*.

THESE GANGS ATTRACT TOUGH ADOLESCENTS WHO USE WEAPONS TO WIN RESPECT FROM RIVALS AND WHO ENGAGE IN UNPREDICTABLE AND DESTRUCTIVE ASSAULTS ON PEOPLE AND PROPERTY.

LET'S DO IT FOR JOHNNY!

PSSST! GUYS! THIS WAY!

THEY MUST BE READY TO FIGHT TO PROTECT THEIR OWN AND THEIR GANG'S INTEGRITY AND HONOR.

A *RETREATIST SUBCULTURE* APPEARS WHEN YOUNG PEOPLE ARE "DOUBLE FAILURES": THEY HAVEN'T BEEN ABLE TO ACHIEVE STATUS THROUGH EITHER LEGITIMATE OR ILLEGITIMATE MEANS.

THEY TEND TO USE DRUGS AND ALCOHOL BECAUSE THEY CAN'T FIND A PLACE IN EITHER CONVENTIONAL SETTINGS OR IN CRIMINAL OR CONFLICT SUBCULTURES.

...taverns...

RESPECT SHOULD BE MAINTAINED AT ALL COST, EVEN IF IT MEANS USING VIOLENCE.

RESPECT, OR "PROPS," IS VERY IMPORTANT--IF A PERSON THINKS HE OR SHE IS BEING "DISSED," THERE CAN BE TROUBLE.

MINOR DISPUTES CAN SNOWBALL INTO VIOLENT EPISODES.

..."stop and go" establishments...

HOWEVER, SINCE DECENT FAMILIES LIVE IN THE COMMUNITY WITH STREET FAMILIES, THEY NEED TO ADAPT BY LEARNING AND OBSERVING THE *CODE OF THE STREET.*

THIS SORT OF ACTIVITY FITS INTO WHAT STREET FAMILIES REALLY BELIEVE. IT'S LIKE THEIR INTERNAL VALUE SYSTEM. BUT GOES AGAINST WHAT DECENT FAMILIES BELIEVE.

AND SO THEY DON'T BECOME VICTIMS, DECENT FAMILIES WILL SOMETIMES "CODE-SWITCH" SO IT LOOKS LIKE THEY FOLLOW TO THE STREET SUBCULTURAL VALUE SYSTEM--BUT DEEP DOWN THEY DON'T.

...and the homes of many gracious individuals.

WHY HAS THIS HAPPENED, YOU WONDER. WELL, IT GOES BACK TO THE FEELINGS OF ALIENATION AND ISOLATION.

IN PARTICULAR, WE DON'T TRUST THAT THE POLICE WILL HELP US, SO WE ARE PERSONALLY RESPONSIBLE FOR OUR OWN SAFETY.

IF THAT MEANS VIOLENCE, WELL, THEN, THAT'S WHAT HAPPENS.

ALTHOUGH ANDERSON'S WORK FOCUSED ON AFRICAN-AMERICANS, IT SHOULD BE NOTED THAT THE SUBCULTURE OF VIOLENCE CAN RELATE TO A VARIETY OF OTHER DEMOGRAPHICS AND LOCALES.

OTHER RESEARCH FOUND EXISTENCE OF A SUBCULTURE OF VIOLENCE IN THE AMERICAN SOUTH, AND AMONG ATHLETES, MIDDLE SCHOOL AND HIGH SCHOOL STUDENTS, AND OTHERS.

23

ACCORDING TO THE FEDERAL BUREAU OF INVESTIGATION, SOME 33,000 VIOLENT STREET GANGS, MOTORCYCLE GANGS, AND PRISON GANGS WITH ABOUT 1.4 MILLION MEMBERS ARE CRIMINALLY ACTIVE IN THE UNITED STATES AND PUERTO RICO TODAY.

ALTHOUGH GANGS HAVE EXPANDED AND EVOLVED DRAMATICALLY SINCE THE DAYS OF THE CLASSIC STUDIES DISCUSSED IN THIS ISSUE, EXPLANATIONS FOR THEIR FORMATION REMAIN MUCH THE SAME.

PEOPLE JOIN GANGS FOR VARIOUS REASONS: STATUS, SECURITY, MONEY, POWER, EXCITEMENT, AND NEW EXPERIENCES.

FOR MANY, SOCIAL INSTITUTIONS (I.E., FAMILY, EDUCATION, ECONOMY) SATISFY MOST NEEDS; BUT FOR SOME, THESE ARE ABSENT, SO A GANG OFFERS AN ATTRACTIVE SUBSTITUTE WAY TO ACHIEVE THOSE NEEDS.

GANG PREVENTION POLICIES SHOULD TRY TO STRENGTHEN SOCIAL INSTITUTIONS AND PROVIDE LEGITIMATE EMPLOYMENT OPPORTUNITIES FOR INDIVIDUALS TO SECURE A LIVING WAGE.

Jobs, not jail
HOMEBOY

UNTIL THEN, IT IS LIKELY THAT GANGS WILL ALWAYS BE A PROBLEM IN THE UNITED STATES.

THIS ISSUE BEGAN WITH AN INTRODUCTION TO THE CONCEPT OF SUBCULTURES IN SOCIETY. DELINQUENT SUBCULTURES HAVE BEEN AN AREA OF INQUIRY FOR MANY CRIMINOLOGISTS SINCE THE 1950S. THESE SUBCULTURAL THEORIES HAVE EVOLVED ALONG VARIOUS DIFFERENT PATHS, AND THIS ISSUE HIGHLIGHTS THOSE PARTICULARLY INFLUENTIAL VERSIONS.

FIRST, A NUMBER OF CRIMINOLOGISTS EXPLORED HOW DELINQUENT SUBCULTURES ARISE IN PARTICULAR SECTORS OF SOCIETY (URBAN LOWER-CLASS AREAS). THESE SUBCULTURES ARE IN EFFECT ADAPTATIONS LOWER-CLASS YOUTH MAKE IN ORDER TO COMPENSATE FOR THE FACT THAT THEY CANNOT LIVE UP TO MAINSTREAM, MIDDLE-CLASS VALUES. ALBERT COHEN PROPOSED THAT LOWER-CLASS YOUTH EXPERIENCE STATUS FRUSTRATION BECAUSE THEY CANNOT ACHIEVE MIDDLE-CLASS STATUS. THE SOLUTION WAS TO CREATE THEIR OWN VALUE SYSTEM THAT WOULD BE THE MEANS BY WHICH UNSUCCESSFUL YOUTH COULD GAIN A SENSE OF STATUS AMONG OTHERS WHO HAVE ALSO FAILED TO ACHIEVE STATUS ACCORDING TO MIDDLE-CLASS VALUES. RICHARD CLOWARD AND LLOYD OHLIN PROPOSED THAT DELINQUENT SUBCULTURES WERE A RESULT OF INDIVIDUALS NOT HAVING LEGITIMATE OPPORTUNITIES TO SUCCEED, AND THESE SUBCULTURES TOOK VARIOUS FORMS DEPENDING ON OPPORTUNITIES FOR ILLEGITIMATE MEANS AND WHERE THE YOUTH RESIDED. THEY PROPOSED THE EXISTENCE OF THREE DELINQUENT SUBCULTURES: CRIMINAL SUBCULTURES, CONFLICT SUBCULTURES, AND RETREATIST SUBCULTURES. MOBILIZATION FOR YOUTH, A PROGRAM DEVELOPED TO PROVIDE LEGITIMATE OPPORTUNITIES TO YOUTH, WAS BASED ON IDEAS PUT FORTH IN THEIR THEORY.

SECOND, BY CONTRAST, SOME CRIMINOLOGISTS HAVE ASSERTED THAT LOWER-CLASS SUBCULTURE AS A WHOLE—NOT SUBCULTURES WITHIN LOWER-CLASS AREAS—IS RESPONSIBLE FOR GENERATING CRIMINAL BEHAVIOR IN URBAN AREAS. WALTER MILLER PROPOSED THAT URBAN GANG DELINQUENCY IS A PRODUCT OF A DISTINCT LOWER-CLASS SUBCULTURES WHOSE "FOCAL CONCERNS" ENCOURAGE CRIMINAL RATHER THAN CONFORMING BEHAVIOR. THESE LOWER-CLASS FOCAL CONCERNS ARE TROUBLE, TOUGHNESS, SMARTNESS, EXCITEMENT, FATE, AND AUTONOMY.

THIRD, OTHER RESEARCHERS HAVE ARGUED FOR THE EXISTENCE OF A SUBCULTURE OF VIOLENCE. WOLFGANG AND FERRACUTI, FOR EXAMPLE, PROPOSED THAT IN AREAS WHERE THIS SUBCULTURE HAD TAKEN HOLD THERE EXISTED PERMISSIVE ATTITUDES TOWARD THE USE OF VIOLENCE TO RESOLVE CONFLICTS. WHILE WOLFGANG AND FERRACUTI GENERATED THESE IDEAS BY INFERRING FROM HOMICIDE DATA, ELIJAH ANDERSON DISCOVERED EVIDENCE OF A SUBCULTURE OF VIOLENCE DURING HIS ETHNOGRAPHIC WORK IN INNER-CITY PHILADELPHIA. HERE THERE EXISTED A CODE OF THE STREET THAT DICTATED BEHAVIOR IN PUBLIC SPACES THAT EMPHASIZED RESPECT AND CONDONED THE USE OF VIOLENCE IF ONE WAS DISRESPECTED OR THREATENED.

Key Terms

Subcultures
Delinquent Subcultures
Gangs
Chicago School
Albert Cohen
Robert Merton
Edwin Sutherland
Macro-Level
Social Psychology
Micro-Level
Middle-Class
Middle-Class Measuring Rod
Status Frustration
Strain
Cultural Transmission
Walter Miller
Special Youth Program (SYP)

Focal Concerns
Trouble
Toughness
Smartness
Excitement
Fate
Autonomy
Differential Opportunity Theory
Illegitimate Means
Criminal Subculture
Conflict Subculture
Retreatist Subculture
Mobilization for Youth
Marvin Wolfgang
Franco Ferracuti
Subculture of Violence
Honor Cultures

Inductive Reasoning
Ethnography
Elijah Anderson
Decent Families
Street Families
Code of the Street

Discussion Questions

Provide modern-day examples of five different subcultures in the United States. Choose one of these subcultures, provide information about their beliefs, attitudes, and behaviors that are distinctive about that subculture, and provide information about what makes their beliefs, attitudes, and behaviors distinctive.

Are low-income delinquents reacting against middle-class values, as Cohen proposes, or is there a low-income culture with its own set of values and attitudes to which delinquents follow, as Miller proposes? Explain your answer.

How do each of the six focal concerns make crime more likely?
Give examples for each.

Have you encountered individuals who seem to engage in behaviors that fit with either Wolfgang and Ferracuti's subculture of violence or Anderson's code of the street? Why do you believe they fit these models?

Suggested Readings

Anderson, E. (1999). *Code of the streets.* New York: W. W. Norton.

Cloward, R., & Ohlin, L. (1960). *Delinquency and opportunity: A theory of delinquent gangs.* New York: Free Press.

Cohen, A. (1955). *Delinquent boys: The culture of the gang.* New York: Free Press.

Cullen, F. T., Agnew, R., & Wilcox, P. (2014). *Criminological theory: Past to present* (5th ed.). New York: Oxford University Press.

Lilly, J. R., Cullen, F. T., & Ball, R. (2015). *Criminological theory: Context and consequences* (6th ed.). Los Angeles: Sage Publications.

Miller, W. (1958). Lower class culture as a generating milieu of gang delinquency. *Journal of Social Issues, 14,* 5–19.

Wolfgang, M., & Ferracuti, F. (1967). *The subculture of violence: Towards an integrated theory in criminology.* London: Tavistock.